SEAWEED

Published by: Cross Media Ltd.
66-67 Wells Street, London W1T 3QB, UK
Tel: 020-7436-1960   Fax: 020-7436-1930

Copyright of Photography and Text © Cross Media Ltd. 2002

Project Manager: Kazuhiro Marumo
Editor: Yoko Takechi
Designer: Misa Watanabe
Photographer: Naomi Igawa, Hiroshi Mitani, Akira Kawai, Naoko Morine
Chef: Miyoko Yoshimura (Akasha Cooking School)
Coordinator: Asahiko Goto. Thanks to: Anthony Nott, Mary Thompson

ISBN 1-897701-04-7
Printed in Japan

All about seaweed

The staple food that keeps you in good health

The history of seaweed (as a food) in Japan dates back to 600 BC. It appears that people in those days ate seaweed as a source of salt, as they had no way of refining salt at that time. By the eighth century, several different types of seaweed were being used as a form of tax to the government, and it was also a popular offering to temples and shrines. When there were very bad harvests in medieval Japan, seaweed was eaten as an alternative to vegetables and was considered to be a precious source of minerals and vitamins. Since that time, various types of seaweed dishes have been created, many of which are eaten as part of the Japanese diet (e.g. miso soup with wakame, sushi with nori (dried seaweed) and various kinds of side dishes using konbu(kelp)). It is further gaining in popularity as it contains virtually no calories and is a good choice for people who are trying to lose weight.

Seaweed and nutrition

A great Japanese health booster!

What is noteworthy about seaweed is that it is particularly rich in minerals and dietary fibre. Minerals help the systems of the body to work properly and most types of seaweed contain 16 essential minerals such as iron, iodine and calcium.

Iodine (an important component of kelp) is helpful in treating hair loss whereas hijiki (which contains 14 times as much calcium as milk) can help to soothe an irritation. Nori also contains Vitamin B1 and B2, which can help prevent ageing. It is also a good food to include in a weight-controlling diet as it is virtually non calorific.

Seaweed – a good source of roughage

Dietary fibre expands in the bowel preventing the food from touching the walls. This slows down the rate at which sugar is absorbed by the body, which can help to prevent diabetes in addition to arteriosclerosis as the storage of cholesterol is delayed. It is also helpful in the prevention of bowel cancer.

4

Types of Seaweed

Rich variety from the gardens of the sea

Types of Seaweed

There are hundreds of different types of seaweed. The following are some of the most common;

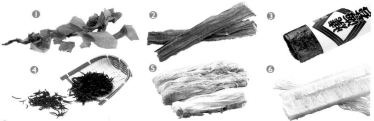

❶ Wakame
Very dark green algae sold dried or moist and salted. It is very popular ingredient in miso soup.

❷ Konbu (kelp)
Sold in thick dried black strips. It is often used to make Japanese soup stock.

❸ Nori
Flat blade-shaped red seaweed that turns black or very dark when dried. It is normally sold in sheets.

❹ Hijiki
A dark brown seaweed that turns black when dried and looks like a short length of wire.

❺ Tororo konbu (vinegared sticky kelp)
Soft pieces of konbu, normally vinegared and shredded.

❻ Kanten (agar)
It is originally a bright red seaweed but is available in powdered form or as a bar. Used as a gelling agent.

How to make Japanese soup stock

One of the key ingredients in Japanese dishes is the soup stock:

Dashi - the basic Japanese soup stock

There are several types of popular dashi but the one made from kelp and bonito flakes is a good choice as it has a mild and smooth flavour and can be used in the same way as chicken stock in western cooking.
Learn this simple recipe and gradually increase your knowledge of Japanese food!

Makes 1 litre

1 sheet of dried kelp
(10cm x 10cm)

1 litre water

15g bonito flakes

1 Make a few slits in the kelp, and cook in water on a medium heat. Remove just before boiling.

2 Add the bonito flakes to the pan, bring to the boil, and strain.

*for vegetarians, use twice as much kelp and omit the bonito.

6

Other ingredients for dashi

Instant dashi

Another popular ingredient for dashi is iriko (often called niboshi) - dried sardine. This is especially suitable for soup dishes (miso soup, noodle soup etc.). Dried shiitake mushrooms are also commonly used and dashi made from chicken, beef or pork are other good choices. Various kinds of instant dashi are also available in sachets, liquid and powdered form.

Iriko   Shiitake

How to make shiitake dashi   - perfect for vegetarians!

Makes I litre

5-6 dried shiitake
mushrooms

I litre water

Simply place the mushrooms in the water, leave for at least I hour, then strain. If you do not have time, boil once and leave for 10 minutes.

Thick Rolled Sushi

太巻き *Futo-maki*

Choose your favourite filling!

Makes 1 roll

120g rice
180ml water
½ egg, lightly beaten
1 tsp sugar
30g spinach
3 crabsticks
1 sheet *nori*
(19 × 21 cm)

* See page 6 how to cook soup stock

1. Cook rice in the water. Put it in the flat-bottomed bowl. Mix [A] and pour it into the rice. Mix the rice with a spatula, taking care not to mash it, but making sure that all the vinegar is absorbed. Cool the rice down with a paper fan.

[A]

1 tbsp rice vinegar

1 tsp sugar

a pinch of salt

[B]

250ml Japanese soup stock

1 tbsp sugar

1 tbsp soy sauce

2 tsp *mirin*

10g gourd (cut in ribbons)

2 Boil the spinach lightly and drain. Add 1 tsp sugar to the beaten egg and make a very thin omelette. Cut it into very thin strips, 2 mm in width.

3  Rinse the gourd; rub it with salt, and soak it in lukewarm water for 10 minutes, then boil it for 5 minutes. Mix it in a pan with [B], bring to the boil, then lower the heat and cook for 15 minutes.

4 Place the *nori* on a bamboo rolling mat (If you do not have one, use a sheet of cling film), and spread the rice over the *nori*, leaving 1 cm free on the near side and 2 cm on the opposite side.

Tip!

To make a good round shape, roll it in one go and then form it by pressing gently.

5 Place the filling down the centre.

6 Put your thumbs at the back of the mat and roll it to wrap the rice in nori.

7 Cut into 2 cm slices with a damp knife.

Hand Rolled Salad

● 手巻きサラダ *Temaki Sarada* ●

Serves 2

[fillings]
¼ cucumber
½ carrot
some cress
1 egg
2 slices of ham
50g cheese
150g tinned tuna
3-4 sheets of *nori*
(19 × 21 cm),
cut into quarters

[dipping sauce A]
1 tbsp ground sesame
2 tsp soy sauce
1 tsp rice vinegar

[dipping sauce B]
3 tbsp mayonnaise
1 tsp *wasabi*
1 tsp soy sauce

1 Make a very thin omelette from the egg. Cut the cucumber, carrot, ham and omelette into thin strips, 5-6 cm in length. Remove the oil from the tinned tuna.

2 Lay out the fillings and *nori* on separate plates. Mix the ingredients for each dipping sauce.

3 Put the fillings of your choice on a sheet of *nori*, roll it up, and eat!

Tempura with Seaweed Flavour

● 磯辺揚げ *Isobe-age* ●

2 types of Tempura with a taste from the ocean.

Serves 2

150g *kabocha* pumpkin

150g sweet potato

100g plain flour

1 egg

150ml chilled water

½ sheet *nori* (20 × 10 cm)

* See page 6 how to make soup stock

1 Cut the pumpkin and sweet potato into thin slices, 4-5 mm in width. Crush the *nori* into very small pieces.

. . . .

1.5 tsp *ao-nori*

some vegetable oil
for deep-frying

[dipping sauce]

200ml Japanese
soup stock

50ml soy sauce

50ml *mirin*

2

Beat the egg in a bowl. Add
the flour and water, and mix
well.

3 Transfer half the batter to
another bowl and mix with
the *nori*. Mix the remaining
batter with the *ao-nori*.

4 Heat the oil in a deep pan to 180°C.

Tip!

To make light and crispy tempura, chill the water, egg and flour before use.

5 Dip the vegetables into either type of batter and deep-fry until they float on the surface of the oil. Place them on a kitchen towel to remove any excess oil.

6 Put the ingredients of the sauce in a pan and bring to the boil. Place the tempura on a plate and serve with a bowl of the dipping sauce.

Rolled Chicken in Konbu

● 鶏の昆布巻き *Tori no Konbu-maki* ●

A traditional Japanese family dish.
Try using root vegetables instead of chicken.

Serves 4

30g dried *konbu*

200ml water

200g chicken thigh
or breast

20cm gourd

600ml Japanese
soup stock

* See page 6 how to cook soup stock

1. Soak the *konbu* in the water.
Keep the water to use later.
Rinse the gourd, rub it with
salt and soak in lukewarm
water. Cut it into 8 cm strips.

Konbu-maki

. . . .

[A]
1 tbsp sugar
4 tbsp *sake*
2 tbsp *mirin*
3 tbsp soy sauce

2 Cut the *konbu* into rectangular strips, 5 × 10 cm.

3

Cut the chicken into thin strips (the same number as the *konbu*), 5cm in length.

4 Place a strip of chicken on the *konbu*, along the narrow side, and roll toward the other end. Then tie the centre of the roll with a strip of gourd. Repeat the process until you have used up all the *konbu*.

. . . .

Tip!

If you don't have any gourd, use short skewers to keep the konbu and chicken together.

5 Place the rolled konbu in a pan, and add the soup stock and the water used for soaking it.

6 Cut the cooking foil slightly smaller than the pan in diameter and cover the konbu with it. Simmer until the konbu becomes soft.

7 Add [A] to the pan and simmer again for about 15 minutes.

20

Stir Fried Beef with Konbu

昆布と牛肉の炒めもの *Konbu to gyuniku no Itamemono*

Serves 2

10g dried *konbu*

100g thin sliced beef

2 tsp *sake*

2 tsp soy sauce

2 tsp corn or
potato flour

1 piece of garlic,
chopped

½ green pepper

50g tinned
bamboo shoots

sesame oil
for stir-frying

[A]

1 tbsp soy sauce

1 tbsp *sake*

1 tsp sugar

1 Soak the *konbu* in water for 10 minutes then cut into very fine strips, 5 cm in length. Cut the beef, pepper and bamboo shoot into fine strips. Rub the *sake*, soy sauce and corn flour onto the beef.

2 Heat the oil in a frying pan. Stir fry the garlic followed by the beef. When the meat has changed colour, remove from the pan and put to one side.

3 Add more oil to the pan and stir-fry the *konbu* and vegetables. Once they are cooked, put the beef back in the pan and season with [A].

Lightly Pickled Vegetables

浅漬け　*Asa-zuke* ●

Seves 4

½ cucumber

10 cm *daikon*

[pickle]

5 x 15 cm *konbu*

70ml rice vinegar

100ml water

1.5 tsp salt

2 tbsp *sake*

2 tbsp sugar

2 tsp soy sauce

⅓ red chili pepper, chopped

1 Cut the cucumber length-ways in four, then cut into bite size pieces. Cut *daikon* in the same way.

2 Place the ingredients for the pickle in a pan and bring to the boil.

3 Put the vegetables in a lidded container and pour in the pickle. For the best flavour, eat 2-5 days after preparation.

Wakeme Salad with Sesami Dressing

わかめサラダ ごま風味 *Wakame Sarada Goma Fūmi*

Serves 2

5g dried *wakame*

¼ onion

2 tomatoes

80g silken *tōfu* (¼ standard size block)

[dressing sauce]

2 tsp ground sesame

1.5 tbsp mayonnaise

1 tsp sesame oil

1 tsp lemon juice

some Japanese mustard (optional)

1. Soak the *wakame* in water to revitalize, and cut into bite size pieces. Cut the onion and tomatoes into thin slices. Cut *tōfu* into 2 cm cubes.

2. Spread the tomato on the plate. Mix the *wakame*, onion and tofu together and place on the tomatoes.

3. Mix the ingredients for the dressing sauce together and pour on the salad just before serving.

Wakame Soup

- わかめスープ　*Wakame Sūpu* -

Serves 2

10g dried *wakame*

1 egg

8 mange tout

300ml Japanese soup stock

2 tsp *sake*

some salt and pepper

* See page 6 how to cook soup stock

1   Soak the *wakame* in water to revitalize and cut into bite size pieces. Trim the mange tout and put quickly in boiling water.

2   Place the soup stock and *sake* in a pan, bring to the boil, add the *wakame* and mange tout, and season with salt and pepper.

3   Just before removing the pan from the heat, pour in the beaten egg and stir.

Rolled Omelette with Wakame

わかめ入り厚焼き卵　*Wakame-iri Atsuyaki Tamago*

Makes 1 roll

4 eggs
3g dried *wakame*
some vegetable oil

[A]
3 tbsp sugar
2 tsp *mirin*
1 tsp soy sauce
a pinch of salt

1 Soak the *wakame* in water and then cut into very small pieces. Mix the eggs with [A] in a bowl and add the *wakame*.

2 Pour a small quantity of the egg in a greased frying pan and spread it over to cover the pan thinly. When half cooked, roll it towards one side of the pan. Pour more egg into the pan, and repeat the process in the other direction.

3

Repeat the rolling procedure until the mixture is used up. Then put the cooked egg into a bamboo rolling mat, shaping it into a rectangle. Once it has cooled, cut into pieces, 2 cm in width.

Seafood Spaghetti

シーフードスパゲティ　*Shifūdo Supageti*

A gorgeous seafood concoction!

Serves 2

5g *wakame*
70g squid
70g small prawns
8 mussels (in shells)
180g spaghetti

1. Soak the *wakame* to revitalize and cut into bite size pieces. Cut the squid into bite size strips. Rinse the mussels in salted water.

some olive oil

1 tbsp butter

2 tbsp *sake* or white wine

2 tbsp soy sauce some salt and pepper

some *nori*, cut into very fine strips

2

Cook the spaghetti in plenty of water (slightly salted), then drain and sprinkle with olive oil.

3 Pour the *sake* in a frying pan (if it is not enough to cover the bottom of the pan, add some more). Add butter, salt and pepper, then all the seafood. Cover with a lid and steam until the mussels open.

33

Tip!

To save time you can use frozen mixed seafood

4 Add the spaghetti to the seafood (keeping it on the heat) and season with soy sauce, salt and pepper.

5 Add the *wakame* just before removing the pan from the heat.

6 Dish up the spaghetti and sprinkle on the *nori* just before serving.

Simmered Hijiki

ひじきの煮物　*Hijiki no Nimono*

A rich tasting dish that goes well with plain rice, and can be kept in the fridge for 3-4 days.

Serves 2

30g dried *hijiki*

1 thin fried bean curd

½ carrot

150ml Japanese soup stock

2 tbsp sugar

* See page 6 how to cook soup stock

1 Rinse the *hijiki* well until the water runs clear, then soak in plenty of water for 30 minutes. Cut into bite size pieces.

1 tbsp *sake*
2 tbsp soy sauce

2

Put the fried bean curd in a sieve and pour boiling water through it to remove excess oil. Cut in half lengthways and into fine strips.

3 Cut the carrot into very fine strips.

Hijiki no Nimono

Tip!

Take enough time to soak the *hijiki* or it won't absorb enough broth when simmering.

4 Place the *hijiki*, bean curd and carrot in a pan, add the soup stock, suger and *sake*, and bring to a boil.

5

Cut the cooking foil slightly smaller than the pan in diameter and cover the *hijiki* with it. Simmer for 5 minutes.

6 Add the soy sauce, and simmer again until the *hijiki* absorbs the broth.

Ground Tofu with Hijiki

● ひじきの白あえ *Hijiki no Shiro-ae* ●

Serves 2

80g simmered *hijiki**
½ cotton *tōfu*
(½ standard size)
1 tbsp ground sesame
1.5 tbsp sugar
2 tsp *mirin*
a pinch of salt

* See page 36 how to cook simmered *hijiki*

1 Wrap the *tōfu* in a tea towel and place a plate or a bowl on top to force out excess water. Leave for about 15 minutes.

2 Grind the sesame and *tōfu* with a mortar and pestle (If you do not have them, use a bowl and fork) and mix with the sugar, *mirin* and salt.

3 Add the simmered *hijiki* to the *tōfu* mixture and mix well.

Tororo Konbu Soup

● とろろ昆布汁 *Tororo Kombu-jiru* ●

Serves 2

a handful of
tororo konbu

400ml Japanese
Soup Stock

1 tbsp soy sauce

½ tsp ground ginger

1 tsp *sake*

1 chive

* See page 6 how to cook soup stock

1   Chop the chive into small
pieces.

2   Heat the soup stock. When it
has come to the boil, slightly
lower the heat and add
tororo konbu, ginger, soy
sauce and *sake*.

3   When it comes to the boil again, remove from the heat.
Garnish with the chopped chive.

Rice Ball with Tororo Konbu

● おにぎりのとろろ昆布巻 *Onigiri no Tororo Konbu-maki* ●

Makes 4

a handful of
tororo konbu

400g cooked rice

some soy sauce

[filling]

Choose from
the following:

salted salmon,

pickled plums,

tinned tuna
with mayonnaise,

cod roe etc.

1 Wet the palms of your hands. Spread a quarter of the rice in the palm of one hand, making a small hollow for the filling in the centre.

2 Add the filling and shape the rice in a triangular form. Repeat the process four times.

3 Spread the soy sauce thinly over each ball and wrap with *tororo konbu*.

Almond Curd

● 杏仁豆腐 *Annin-dōfu* ●

4g powdered
kanten

50g sugar

200ml water

300ml milk or
soya milk

2-3 drops of
almond essence

A tin of fruit
cocktail (450g)

1 Place the *kanten* and water in a pan and bring to the boil, stirring constantly. Lower the heat and simmer for 2 minutes. Add milk and bring to the boil again.

2 Remove the pan from the heat and add the almond essence. Pour the mixture into a damp tub and refrigerate.

3

When it is set, cut into small oval shaped pieces and serve with the tinned fruit and its syrup.

• Guide to ingredients - Seaweed •

Abura-age	fried bean curd
Ao-nori	green seaweed flakes
Daikon	Japanese radish
Dashi	Japanese soup stock
kabocha	Japanese pumpkin
Kampyō	edible gourd
Katsuobushi	bonito flakes
Komezu	rice vinegar
Mirin	cooking sake (sweet)
Niboshi	dried sardine
Sake	Japanese rice wine
	auce
	d sesame
	)e
	urd
	plum
	e horseradish